Flowers

Flowers

David Hamilton

PAVILION

First published in Great Britain in 1990 by
PAVILION BOOKS LIMITED
196 Shaftesbury Avenue, London WC2H 8JL
Photograph copyright © 1990 David Hamilton
copyright © 1990 L'Ariana Pictures - Paris
Designed by David Hamilton

A CIP catalogue record for this book is
available from the British Library

ISBN 185145 442X
10 9 8 7 6 5 4 3 2 1
Printed and bound in Italy
by Mondadori (Verona)

*ON THE OPPOSITE PAGE SWINBURNE'S POEM
"SPRING BEGINS" CALLIGRAPHED BY SARAH LOGAN,
COURTESY OF EDITIONS ALAIN MAZERAN, PARIS.*

And time remembered
is grief forgotten
And frosts are slain
and flowers begotten
And in green underwood and cover
Blossom by blossom
the spring begins.

Swinburne

INTRODUCTION

I have been photographing flowers for over twenty years. What attracted me to flowers? Their innate beauty, obviously; their texture, the subtlety and variety of colours; their sensuality and serenity. Over this same period of time I've also been photographing landscapes and still lifes, again looking for these same elements of timelessness. That in fact is what drew me to Venice, where I stayed for a long time getting to know the unchanging heart and soul of that unique city. I would hope that a sixteenth- or seventeenth-century Venetian, viewing my photographs of Venice, would feel perfectly familiar with them.

I see my flowers as having both a natural and a painterly quality. That may sound contradictory, but really it is not. I like flowers in their natural state, not arranged, or in vases: I try to break down the everyday bouquet. And in photographing them I resort to utter simplicity from a technical viewpoint. one camera, one lens, only daylight. "Simplicity" is the key, the very opposite of a studio set-up, with lighting and style and all the technology that goes with it.

One of my masters of photography is Robert Demachy, the leading exponent of the pictorialist movement at the end of the nineteenth century. He photographed like a painter. In truth, art has been a greater source of inspiration to me than photography. I greatly admire the style of Puvis de Chavannes, the way he handled his subjects; the landscapes of Turner, who was the world's first impressionist; the still lifes of Giorgio Morandi; the nudes of Balthus, with their delicate sensuality; the fruits of Chardin; the flowers of Fantin-Latour.

I photographed some of these flowers in exotic places around the world — Mauritius Islands, Hawaii, Thailand, the Philippines, Japan, even Guam — but many were shot right in my own backyard, so to speak, that is, at my home in the south of France.

Each of the pictures represents a particular moment in my life: some are from yesterday, others are two decades old, but all are there, in their beauty and elegance, fresh and sensuous, their colours and textures untouched by time.

David HAMILTON

Flowers to the fair! To you these flowers I bring,
And strive to greet you with an earlier spring.
Flowers sweet, and gay, and delicate like you;
Emblems of innocence, and beauty too.
With flowers the Graces bind their yellow hair,
And flowering wreaths consenting lovers wear.
Flowers, the sole luxury which nature knew,
In Eden's pure and guiltless garden grew.

ANNA LAETITIA BARBAULD FROM "TO A LADY WITH SOME PAINTED FLOWERS"

Coming to kiss her lyps (such grace I found)
Me seemed I smelt a gardin of sweet flowers,
That dainty odours from them threw around,
For damzels fit to decke their lovers' bowres.

EDMUND SPENSER

Shall I compare thee to a summer's day?
Thou art more lovely and more temperate:
Rough winds to shake the darling buds of May,
And summer's lease hath all too short a date:
Sometimes too hot the eye of heaven shines,
And often is his gold complexion dimm'd,
And every fair from fair sometimes declines,
By chance or nature's changing course untrimm'd:
But thy eternal summer shall not fade
Nor lose possession of that fair thou ow'st,
Nor shall Death brag thou wander'st in his shade,
When in eternal lines to time thou grow'st:
So long as men can breathe or eyes can see,
So long lives this, and this gives life to thee.

WILLIAM SHAKESPEARE "SHALL I COMPARE THEE TO A SUMMER'S DAY?"

All nature's ways are mysteries! Endless youth
Lives in them all, unchangeable as truth.
With the odd number five, her curious laws
Play many freaks, nor once mistake the cause;
For in the cowslip-peeps this very day
Five spots appear, which Time wears not away,
Nor once mistakes in counting - look within
Each peep, and five, nor more nor less, are seen.
So trailing bindweed, with its pinky cup,
Five leaves of paler hue go streaking up;
And many a bird, too, keeps the rule alive,
Laying five eggs, nor more nor less than five.
But flowers, how many own that mystic power,
With five leaves ever making up the flower!

I have a love for flowers:
Guess you not why? Their roots are in the earth,
And, when the dead awake or talk in sleep,
These hear their thoughts and write them on their leaves
For heaven to look on: and their dews come down
From the deep bosom of the blue, whereon
The spirits linger, sent by them perchance
With blessings to their friends. Besides all night
They are wide-awaking, and the ghosts will pause,
And breathe their thoughts upon them.

THOMAS LOVELL BEDDOES FROM "AN APOTHEOSIS"

The flower that smiles to-day
To-morrow dies;
All that we wish to stay
Tempts and then flies.
What is the world's delight?
Lightning that mocks the night,
Brief even as bright.

Virtue, how frail it is!
Friendship how rare!
Love, how it sells poor bliss
For proud despair!
But we, though soon they fall,
Survive their joy, and all
Which ours we call.

Whilst skies are blue and bright,
Whilst flowers are gay,
Whilst eyes that change ere night
Makes glad the day;
Whilst yet the calm hours creep,
Dream thou - and from thy sleep
Then wake to weep.

PERCY BYSSHE SHELLEY "MUTABILITY"

Thanks to the human heart by which we live,
Thanks to its tenderness, its joys, and fears,
To me the meanest flower that blows can give
Thoughts that do often lie too deep for tears.

WILLIAM WORDSWORTH FROM "INTIMATIONS OF IMMORTALITY"

Beloved, thou hast brought me many flowers
Plucked in the garden, all the summer through
And winter, and it seemed as if they grew
In this close room, nor missed the sun and showers.
So, in the like name of that love of ours,
Take back these thoughts, which here unfolded too,
And which on warm and cold days I withdrew
From my heart's ground.
ELIZABETH BARRETT BROWNING FROM "SONNETS FROM THE PORTUGUESE"

I *am tired of tears and laughter,*
And men that laugh and weep;
Of what may come hereafter
For men that sow to reap:
I am weary of days and hours,
Blown buds of barren flowers,
Desires and dreams and powers
And everything but sleep.

Hesperus the day is gone
Soft falls the silent dew
A tear is now on many a flower
And heaven lives in you

Hesperus the closing flower
Sleeps on the dewy ground
While dews fall in a silent shower
And heaven breathes around

Look at the fate of Summer flowers,
Which blow at daybreak, droop ere evensong;
And, grieved at their brief date, confess that ours,
Measured by what we are, and ought to be,
Measured by all that trembling we foresee,
Is not so long.

I sent thee late a rosy wreath,
Not so much honouring thee
As giving it a hope that there
It could not withered be;
But thou thereon didst only breathe,
And sent'st it back to me;
Since when it grows, and smells, I swear,
Not of itself, but thee.

BEN JONSON FROM "TO CELIA"

Oh how much more doth beauty beauteous seem
By that sweet ornament which truth doth give!
The rose looks fair, but fairer it we deem
For that sweet odour which doth in it live.
The canker blooms have full as deep a dye
As the perfumed tincture of the roses,
Hang on such thorns and play as wantonly
When summer's breath their masked buds discloses:
But for their virtue only is their show
They live unwoo'd and unrespected fade -
Die to themselves. Sweet roses do not so;
Of their sweet deaths are sweetest odours made:
And so of you, beauteous and lovely youth,
When that shall fade, by verse distills your truth.

WILLIAM SHAKESPEARE "OH HOW MUCH MORE DOTH BEAUTY BEAUTEOUS SEEM"

But when the melancholy fit shall fall
Sudden from heaven like a weeping cloud,
That fosters the droop-headed flowers all,
And hides the green hill in an April shroud;
Then glut thy sorrow on a morning rose,
Or on the rainbow of the salt sand-wave,
Or on the wealth of globed peonies;
Or if thy mistress some rich anger shows,
Emprison her soft hand, and let her rave,
And feed deep, deep upon her peerless eyes.

Gorgeous flowerets in the sunlight shining,
Blossoms flaunting in the eye of day,
Tremulous leaves with soft and silver lining,
Buds that open only to decay;

Brilliant hopes, all woven in gorgeous tissues,
Flaunting gaily in the golden light,
Large desires, with most uncertain issues,
Tender wishes, blossoming at night!

F*ull many a flower is born to blush unseen,*
And waste its sweetness on the desert air.

Now sleeps the crimson petal, now the white;
Nor waves the cypress in the palace walk;
Nor winks the gold fin in the porphyry font:
The fire-fly wakens: waken thou with me.

Now droops the milkwhite peacock like a ghost,
And like a ghost she glimmers on to me.

Now lies the Earth all Danae to the stars,
And all thy heart lies open up to me.

Now slides the silent meteor on, and leaves
A shining furrow, as thy thoughts in me.

Now folds the lily all her sweetness up,
And slips into the bosom of the lake:
So fold thyself, my dearest, thou, and slip
Into my bosom and be lost in me.

ALFRED, LORD TENNYSON "NOW SLEEPS THE CRIMSON PETAL"

ROBERT BROWNING "IN A GONDOLA"

How fresh, O Lord, how sweet and clean
Are thy returns! ev'n as the flowers in spring;
To which, besides their own demean,
The late-past frosts tributes of pleasure bring.
Grief melts away
Like snow in May,
As if there were no such cold thing.

All the letters I can write
Are not as fair as this -
Syllables of Velvet -
Sentences of Plush,
Depths of Ruby, undrained,
Hid, Lip, for Thee -
Play it were a Humming Bird -
And just sipped - me -

The whiles some one did chaunt this lovely lay;
Ah see, who so faire thing doest faine to see,
In springtime flowre the image of thy day;
Ah see the Virgin Rose, how sweetly shee
Doth first peepe forth with bashfull modestee,
The fairer seemes, the lesse ye see her may;
Lo see soone after, how more bold and free
Her bared bosome she doth broad display;
Loe see soone after, how she fades and falles away.

So passeth, in the passing of a day,
Of mortall life the leafe, the bud, the flowre,
Ne more doth flourish after first decay,
That earst was sought to decke both bed and bowre,
Of many a Ladie, and many a Paramowre:
Gather therefore the Rose, whilst yet is prime,
For soone comes age, that will her pride deflowre:
Gather the Rose of love, whilst yet is time
Whilest loving thou mayst loved be with equall crime.

EDMUND SPENSER FROM "THE FAERIE QUEEN"

Bright Tulips, we do know,
You had your coming hither:
And Fading-time does show,
That ye may quickly wither.

Your Sister-hoods may stay
And smile here for your houre;
But dye ye must away:
Even as the meanest Flower.

Come Virgins then, and see
Your frailties; and bemone ye;
For lost like these, 'twill be,
As time had never known ye.

ROBERT HERRICK "TO A BED OF TULIPS"

But little needs this earth of ours
That shining from above her,
When many Pleiades of flowers
(Not one lost) star her over:
The rays of their unnumbered hues
Being refracted by the dews.

I cannot see what flowers are at my feet,
Nor what soft incense hangs upon the boughs,
But in embalmed darkness, guess each sweet
Wherewith the seasonable month endows
The grass, the thicket, and the fruit-tree wild.

And the hyacinth purple, and white, and blue,
Which flung from its bells a sweet peal anew
Of music so delicate, soft and intense,
It was felt like an odour within the sense.

Sunned in the South, and here to-day;
- If all organic things
Be sentient, Flowers, as some men say,
What are your ponderings?

How can you stay, nor vanish quite
From this bleak spot of thorn
And birch, and fir, and frozen white
Expanse of the forlorn?

Frail luckless exiles hither brought!
Your dust will not regain
Old sunny haunts of Classic thought
When you shall waste and wane;

But mix, with alien earth, be lit
With frigid Boreal flame,
And not a sign remain in it
To tell man whence you came.

We are the sweet Flowers
Born of sunny showers,
Think, whene're you see us, what our beauty saith:
Utterance mute and bright
Of some unknown delight,
We fill the air with pleasure, by our simple breath:
All who see us, love us;
We befit all places;
Unto sorrow we give smiles, and unto graces, graces.

LEIGH HUNT FROM "SONG OF THE FLOWERS"

As then the Tulip for her morning sup
Of Heavenly Vintage from the soil looks up,
Do you devoutly do the like, till Heaven
To Earth invert you - like an empty cup.
EDWARD FITZGERALD FROM "THE RUBIAYAT OF OMAR KHAYYAM"

You'll love me yet - and I can tarry
Your love's protracted growing:
June reared that bunch of flowers you carry,
From seeds of April's sowing.

I plant a heartful now: some seed
At least is sure to strike,
And yield - what you'll not pluck indeed,
Not love, but maybe like.

ROBERT BROWNING FROM "GIRL'S SONG"

If Zeus chose us a King of the flowers in his mirth,
He would call to the rose and would royally crown it,
For the rose, ho, the rose! is the grace of the earth,
Is the light of the plants that are growing upon it.
For the rose, ho, the rose! is the eye of the flowers,
Is the blush of the meadows that feel themselves fair, —
Is the lightning of beauty, that strikes through the bowers
On pale lovers who sit in the glow unaware.
Ho, the rose breathes of love! ho, the rose lifts the cup
To the red guest of Cyprus invoked for a guest!
Ho, the rose having curled its sweet eaves for the world,
Takes delight in the motion its petals keep up,
As they laugh to the Wind as it laughs from the West.

ELIZABETH BARRETT BROWNING "SONG OF THE ROSE" (ATTRIBUTED TO SAPPHO)

Goe lovely Rose,
Tell her that wastes her time and me,
That now she knowes,
When I resemble her to thee
How sweet and fair she seems to be.

Tell her that's young,
And shuns to have her Graces spy'd,
That hadst thou sprung
In Desarts, where no men abide,
Thou must have uncommended dyd'd.

Small is the worth
Of Beauty from the light retir'd:
Bid her come forth,
Suffer her selfe to be desir'd,
And not blush to be admir'd.

Then die, that she
The common fate of all things rare
May read in thee,
How small a part of time they share,
That are so wondrous sweet and fair.

EDMUND WALLER "GOE LOVELY ROSE"

And yet who knows what end the scythed wheat
Makes of its foolish poppies' mouths of red?
These were not sown, these are not harvested,
They grow a month and are cast under feet
And none has care thereof,
As none has care of a divided love.

ALGERNON CHARLES SWINBURNE FROM "BEFORE PARTING"

To see a World in a Grain of Sand
And a heaven in a Wild Flower,
Hold Infinity in the palm of your hand
And Eternity in an hour.

WILLIAM BLAKE FROM "AUGURIES OF INNOCENCE"

I love flowers too; not for a young girl's reason,
But because these brief visitors to us
Rise yearly from the neighbourhood of the dead,
To show us how far fairer and more lovely
Their world is; and return thither again,
Like parting friends that beckon us to follow,
And lead the way silent and smilingly.
Fair is the season when they come to us,
Unfolding the delights of that existence
Which is below us: 'tis the time of spirits,
Who with the flowers, and, like them, leave their graves:
But when the earth is sealed, and none dare come
Upwards to cheer us, and man's left alone,
We have cold cutting winter.

THOMAS LOVELL BEDDOES "THE LOVE OF FLOWERS"

Methought that of these visionary flowers
I made a nosegay, bound in such a way
That the same hues which in their natural bowers
Were mingled or opposed, like the array
Kept these imprison'd children of the Hours
Within my hand; - and then, elate and gay,
I hasten'd to the spot whence I had come,
That I might there present it - O! to whom?

PERCY BYSSHE SHELLEY FROM "THE QUESTION"

Come, ye fair, ambrosial flowers,
Leave your beds, and leave your bowers,
Blooming, beautiful and rare,
Form a posy for my fair;
Fair, and bright, and blooming be,
Fit for such a nymph as she.

Nothing is so beautiful as spring -
When weeds, in wheels, shoot long and lovely and lush;
Thrush's eggs look little low heavens, and thrush
Through the echoing timber does so rinse and wring
The ear, it strikes like lightnings to hear him sing;
The glassy peartree leaves and blooms, they brush
The descending blue; that blue is all in a rush
With richness; the racing lambs too have fair their fling.

What is all this juice and all this joy?
A strain of the earth's sweet being in the beginning
In Eden garden. - Have, get, before it cloy,
Before it cloud, Christ, lord, and sour with sinning,
Innocent mind and Mayday in girl and boy,
Most, o maid's child, thy choice and worthy be the winning.

GERARD MANLEY HOPKINS "SPRING"

There never yet was flower fair in vain,
Let classic poets rhyme it as they will...
Nor is a true soul ever born for naught
Wherever any such hath bloomed and died.

JAMES RUSSELL LOWELL FROM "SONNET"

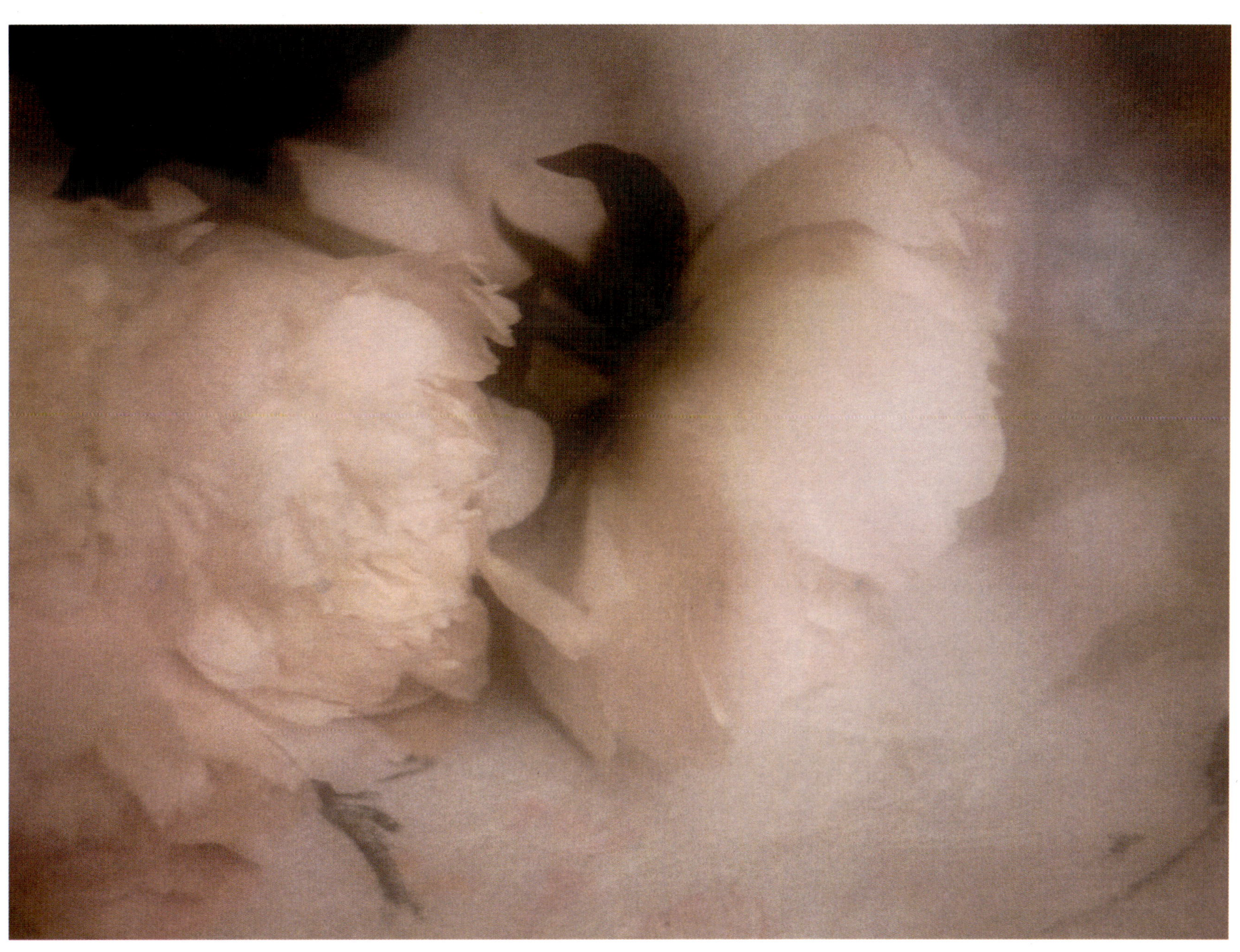

All things that pass
Are woman's looking-glass;
They show her how her bloom must fade,
And she herself be laid
With withered roses in the shade;
With withered roses and the fallen peach,
Unlovely, out of reach
Of summer joy that was.

All things that pass
Are woman's tiring-glass;
The faded lavender is sweet,
Sweet the dead violet
Culled and laid by and cared for yet;
The dried-up violets and dried lavender
Still sweet may comfort her,
Nor need she cry Alas!

All things that pass
Are wisdom's looking-glass;
Being full of hope and fear, and still
Brimful of good or ill,
According to our work and will;
For there is nothing new beneath the sun;
Our doings have been done,
And that which shall be was.

CHRISTINA ROSSETTI "PASSING AND GLASSING"

Partake as doth the Bee,
Abstemiously.
The Rose is an Estate -
In Sicily.

EMILY DICKINSON "PARTAKE AS DOTH THE BEE"

Sweet flowers; - what living eye hath viewed
Their myriads? - endlessly renewed,
Wherever the subtle waters stray;
Wherever sportive zephyrs bend
Their course, or genial showers descend!
Mortals rejoice! the very angels quit
Their mansions unsusceptible of change,
Amid your pleasant bowers to sit,
And through your sweet vicissitudes to range!

WILLIAM WORDSWORTH "RETURN OF SPRING"

Once more the changed year's turning wheel returns:
And as a girl sails balanced in the wind,
And now before and now again behind
Stoops as it swoops, with cheek that laughs and burns, —
So spring comes merry towards me here, but earns
No answering smile from me, whose life is twin'd
With the dead boughs that winter still must bind,
And whom today the spring no more concerns.

Behold this crocus is a withering flame;
This snowdrop, snow; this apple-blossom's part
To bread the fruit to breed the serpent's art.
Nay, for these Spring-flowers, turn thy face from them,
Nor stay till on the year's last lily-stem
The white cup shrivels round the golden heart.

DANTE GABRIEL ROSSETTI "BARREN SPRING"

Love lies beyond
The tomb, the earth, which fades like dew!
I love the fond,
The faithful, and the true.

Love lies in sleep,
The happiness of healthy dreams:
Eve’s dews may weep,
But love delightful seems.

’Tis seen in flowers,
And in the even’s pearly dew;
On earth’s green hours,
And in the heaven’s eternal blue.

’Tis heard in spring
When light and sunbeams, warm and kind,
On angel’s wing
Bring love and music to the mind.

And where is voice,
So young, so beautifully sweet
As nature’s choice,
When spring and lovers meet?

Love lies beyond
The tomb, the earth, the flowers, and dew.
I love the fond,
The faithful, young, and true.

JOHN CLARE "LOVE LIES BEYOND THE TOMB"

Ah, Sunflower, weary of time
Who countest the steps of the sun;
Seeking after that sweet golden clime
Where the traveller's journey is done;

Where the Youth pined away with desire,
And the pale virgin shrouded in snow,
Arise from their graves, and aspire
Where my sunflower wishes to go!

WILLIAM BLAKE "AH, SUNFLOWER"

Farewell, dear flowers, sweetly your time ye spent:
Fit, while ye lived, for smell or ornament,
And after death for cures.
I follow straight without complaint or grief,
Since if my scent be good, I care not, if
It be as short as yours.

GEORGE HERBERT FROM "THE POSY"

As late I rambled in the happy fields,
What time the sky-lark shakes the tremulous dew
From his lush clover-covert; - when anew
Adventurous knights take up their dinted shields:
I saw the sweetest flower wild nature yields,
A fresh-blown musk-rose; 'twas the first that threw
It's sweets upon the summer: graceful it grew
As is the wand that queen Titania wields.
And, as I feasted on its fragrancy,
I thought the garden-rose it far excell'd:
But when, O Wells! thy roses came to me
My sense with their deliciousness was spell'd:
Soft voices had they, that with tender plea
Whisper'd of peace, and truth, and friendliness unquell'd.

Flowers are not flowers unto the poet's eyes,
Their beauty thrills him with an inward sense;
He knows that outward seemings are but lies,
Or, at the most, but earthly shadows, whence
The soul that looks within for truth may guess
The presence of some wondrous heavenliness.

JAMES RUSSELL LOWELL "FLOWERS"

Sweet day, so cool, so calm, so bright,
The bridall of the earth and skie:
The dew shall weep thy fall to night;
For thou must die.

Sweet rose, whose hue angrie and brave
Bids the rash gazer wipe his eye:
Thy root is ever in the grave,
And thou must die.

Onely a sweet and vertuous soul,
Like season'd timber, never gives;
But though the whole world turn to coal,
Then chiefly lives.

GEORGE HERBERT "VERTUE"

O come, dearest Emma, the rose is full blown,
The riches of Flora are lavishly strown,
The air is all softness, and crystal the streams,
The West is resplendently clothed in beams.

O come! let us haste to the freshening shades,
The quaintly carv'd seats, and the opening glades;
Where the faeries are chanting their evening hymns,
And in the sun-beam the sylph lightly swims.

And when thou art weary I'll find thee a bed,
Of mosses and flowers to pillow thy head:
There, beauteous Emma, I'll sit at thy feet,
While my story of love I enraptur'd repeat.

S*outh Winds jostle them -*
Bumblebees come -
Hover - hesitate -
Drink, and are gone -

Butterflies pause
On their passage Cashmere -
I - softly plucking,
Present them here!

EMILY DICKINSON "SOUTH WINDS JOSTLE THEM"

*The flowers left thick at nightfall in the wood
This Eastertide call into mind the men,
Now far from home, who, with their sweethearts, should
Have gathered them and will do never again.*

The garlands fade that Spring so lately wove,
Each simple flower, which she had nurs'd in dew,
Anemonies that spangled every grove,
The primrose wan, and hare-bell, mildly blue.
No more shall violets linger in the dell,
Or purple orchis variegate the plain,
Till Spring again shall call forth every bell,
And dress with humid hands her wreaths again.
Ah! poor humanity! so frail, so fair,
Are the fond vision of thy early day,
Till tyrant passion, and corrosive care,
Bid all thy fairy colours fade away!
Another May new buds and flowers shall bring;
Ah! why has happiness - no second spring?

Brave flowers, that I could gallant it like you,
And be as little vain;
You come abroad, and make a harmless show,
And to your beds of earth again;
You are not proud, you know your birth,
For your embroidered garments are from earth.

You do obey your months, and times, but I
Would ever have it spring,
My fate would know no winter, never die,
Nor think of such a thing;
Oh, that I could my bed of earth but view,
And smile, and look as cheerfully as you.

Oh, teach me to see death, and not to fear,
But rather to take truce;
How often have I seen you at a bier,
And there look fresh and spruce;
You fragrant flowers then teach me, that my breath
Like yours may sweeten and perfume my death.

HENRY KING "A CONTEMPLATION UPON FLOWERS"

When in the east the morning ray
Hangs out the colours of the day,
The bee through these known alley hums
Beating the dian with its drums.
The flowers their drowsy eyelids raise,
Their silken ensigns each displays,
And dries its pan yet dank with dew,
And fills its flask with odours new.

ANDREW MARVELL FROM "UPON APPLETON HOUSE"

A *thing of beauty is a joy for ever:*
Its loveliness increases; it will never
Pass into nothingness; but still will keep
A bower quiet for us, and a sleep
Full of sweet dreams, and health, and quiet breathing.
Therefore, on every morrow we are wreathing
A flowery band to bind us to the earth,
Spite of despondence, of the inhuman dearth
Of noble natures, of the gloomy days
Of all the unhealthy and o'er-darkened ways
Made for our searching: yes, in spite of all,
Some shape of beauty moves away the pall
From our dark spirits.

JOHN KEATS FROM "ENDYMION"

Identification of Flowers:
Page 4   ROSES
Page 9   TULIPS AND RANUNCULUS
Page 11   JASMINE TREE, HIBISCUS AND MADAGASCAR PERIWINKLES
Page 13   PEONIES
Page 15   JASMINE TREE
Page 17   WHITE LISANTHUS
Page 19   PINK LISANTHUS
Page 21   GERMAN IRIS
Page 23   PEONIES
Page 25   JASMINE TREE, HIBISCUS AND MADAGASCAR PERIWINKLES
Page 27   ROSES
Page 29   TULIPS AND RANUNCULUS
Page 31   ROSES AND FLOWERS OF PLUMBAGO
Page 33   ROSES
Page 35   CHINESE PEONIES
Page 37   JASMINE TREE AND HIBISCUS
Page 39   TULIPS
Page 41   TULIPS
Page 43   RANUNCULUS
Page 45   LISANTHUS
Page 47   HIBISCUS
Page 49   ROSES
Page 51   TULIPS
Page 53   GYPSOPHILA OR BABY'S BREATH
Page 55   NIGHT-SCENTED STOCK
Page 57   HYACINTHS
Page 59   GLADIOLUS OR SWORD LILY
Page 61   IRIS
Page 63   TULIPS
Page 65   WHITE-FLOWERED PEONIES
Page 67   ROSES AND ZINNIAS
Page 69   ROSES
Page 71   POPPIES
Page 73   MORNING GLORIES OR IPOMAEA
Page 75   PEONIES
Page 77   HIBISCUS
Page 79   TULIPS
Page 81   TULIPS
Page 83   PEONIES
Page 85   GENISTAS OR BROOM
Page 87   ROSES
Page 89   TULIPS
Page 91   ARUM LILY
Page 93   TULIPS
Page 95   SUNFLOWERS
Page 97   PEONIES
Page 99   ROSES
Page 101 TULIPS
Page 103 ROSES
Page 105 ROSES
Page 107 LISANTHUS
Page 109 PETALS OF ROSES AND FLOWERS OF PLUMBAGO
Page 111 ANEMONES
Page 113 WHITE-FLOWERED PEONIES
Page 115 TULIPS
Page 117 LISANTHUS

Aknowledgments

The idea for this project came from an exhibition at the Grand Palais in Paris, on the occasion of the 'Salon d'automne' *in October 1987, where David Hamilton was the guest of honour. Throughout its evolution,* Flowers *benefited from the friendly support of the Flower Council of Holland, who readily sent us most of the freshly cut tulips and roses which appear here. We would like to pay tribute to them, as well as to their representatives in England, Italy and France, in the piece below.*
We would like to thank the following individuals and companies, without whose assistance that original idea would never have been brought to fruition:
— *Sarah Maguire, for her inspired exploration of English poetry in search of poems to match every floral composition,*
— *The people of 'Pictorial Service' in Paris, who were very attentive in rendering the colours sought by the artist, as well as restoring, with so much passion and patience, originals almost twenty years old,*
— *Jean Larcher for his design of the title,*
— *Bussière Arts Graphiques of Paris, for their outstanding, accurate work in photoengraving,*
— *and, for their enthusiasm and unwavering support of this project, the team at Pavilion Books Ltd., London, and Arcade Publishing, Inc., New York.*
An exhibition of the photographs featured in this book will be presented throughout Europe and in Japan under the sponsorship of prestigious international companies.

Holland: the land of flowers

People the world over associate Holland with flowers and rightly so, since the Dutch people are very partial to fresh blooms and pot plants.
They are an essential item on every Dutch housewife's weekly shopping list and guests at parties rarely arrive without bearing a bunch of beautiful blooms.
You can buy them everywhere - in supermarkets, at the corner stall or from florists and, of course, from the flower market which in most Dutch towns is a weekly or even daily spectacle.
Very early in the morning plants and freshly picked flowers are sent to the numerous auction houses throughout the country where only the very best produce is accepted and anything which falls below their high standards is simply turned away.
As soon as the auctions are over, the plants and flowers are carefully packed in special lorries or aircraft containers and whisked away to their various destinations throughout Holland and abroad.
The conditions and temperatures in which they are kept are closely controlled and invariably Dutch flowers and plants reach their foreign destination on the same day as they are picked.
So you, too, can obtain fresh Dutch flowers or plants at their best.

Floral technical adviser: Marc M. Boers of MARC BOERS - import export of flowers and plants - Aalsmeer, The Netherlands.